Bible Study Series
for senior high

WHY Sharing Faith MATTERS

Loveland, Colorado

Why Sharing Faith Matters
Core Belief Bible Study Series
Copyright © 1998 Group Publishing, Inc.

All rights reserved. No part of this book may be reproduced in any manner whatsoever without prior written permission from the publisher, except where noted in the text and in the case of brief quotations embodied in critical articles and reviews. For information, write Permissions, Group Publishing, Inc., Dept. PD, PO Box 481, Loveland, CO 80539.

Credits
Editor: Julie Meiklejohn
Creative Development Editor: Paul Woods
Chief Creative Officer: Joani Schultz
Copy Editor: Patti Leach
Cover Art Director: Jeff A. Storm
Art Director: Ray Tollison
Computer Graphic Artist/Illustrator: Eris Klein
Photographers: Jafe Parsons and Craig DeMartino
Production Manager: Michelle Kucharski

Unless otherwise noted, Scripture taken from the HOLY BIBLE, NEW INTERNATIONAL VERSION®. Copyright © 1973, 1978, 1984 by International Bible Society. Used by permission of Zondervan Publishing House. All rights reserved.

ISBN 0-7644-0897-6

10 9 8 7 6 5 4 3 2   07 06 05 04 03 02 01 00

Printed in the United States of America.

Visit our Web site: www.grouppublishing.com

Bible Study Series
for senior high

contents:

the Core Belief: Sharing Faith

When our relationship with God grows, a natural result is a desire to share what we have with others. Our motivation to share our faith with others grows out of what God has done for us. We can use all we have at our disposal to communicate God's great love and sacrifice to those who don't know him. We can use our lives by loving others with God's love and living righteous lives. We can communicate God's love through our words by telling our faith stories and telling others about Jesus Christ.

We can't force others to make a commitment to Jesus Christ. Only the Holy Spirit can do the work in people's hearts to give them the desire to give their lives to Christ. But we can do our part. Through the studies in this Core Christian Belief, young people can realize their natural desire to share Christ with those around them. And they can discover how to do this in respectful, loving ways.

the Helpful Stuff

SHARING FAITH AS A CORE CHRISTIAN BELIEF — **7**
(or How to Talk the Talk **and** Walk the Walk)

ABOUT CORE BELIEF BIBLE STUDY SERIES — **10**
(or How to Move Mountains in One Hour or Less)

WHY ACTIVE AND INTERACTIVE LEARNING WORKS WITH TEENAGERS — **57**
(or How to Keep Your Kids Awake)

YOUR EVALUATION — **63**
(or How You Can Edit Our Stuff Without Getting Paid)

the ▼Studies

How to Talk With Others About God
THE ISSUE: Sharing Faith
THE BIBLE CONNECTION: 2 Kings 22:1–23:30 and Philippians 3:2-11
THE POINT: You have to know your story before you can share it.

15

The Joy of the Lord Is My Strength
THE ISSUE: Joy
THE BIBLE CONNECTION: Matthew 5:13-16 and 1 Peter 1:3-9
THE POINT: God can reach others through you.

23

The World Is My Church
THE ISSUE: Global Missions
THE BIBLE CONNECTION: Matthew 25:31-46; 28:18-20; Mark 1:17; Acts 1:8; and Ephesians 6:19
THE POINT: The world needs Jesus.

33

Taking Up the Cross
THE ISSUE: Persecution
THE BIBLE CONNECTION: Psalm 70; Acts 5:12-42; 6:8-10; 7:51-60; 12:1-17; 16:16-34; 2 Corinthians 4:1, 5-7; and 1 Peter 3:15-18
THE POINT: Jesus suffered for us.

47

Sharing Faith as a Core Christian Belief

Sharing your faith in Christ doesn't just mean telling someone how to become a Christian. It can also mean asking God to give you the strength to live a life that would draw someone to him. It means caring for people's needs and leaning on God to give you the right words at the right time. And it means letting the Holy Spirit strengthen you when you've done all you can.

The first study in this book about **sharing faith** will help kids identify their own faith stories and examine the impact God has had on their lives. Kids will learn how to find God's truth in their stories and how to share their own stories with others in practical, natural ways.

In the second study, kids will experience ways they can act as God's instruments through their expressions of **joy** in Christ. This study will help kids realize that they don't always have to "do something" to share their faith with others—sometimes simply living their lives with pure Christian joy is the greatest possible way of sharing faith.

The third study in this book will give kids a deeper awareness of **global missions** while encouraging them to find their own mission fields, whether overseas or in their own hometowns. Kids will understand that the Holy Spirit gives them the power and confidence they need to share Christ with the world.

The fourth study focuses on the issue of **persecution** because of faith. Kids will be motivated to take action in spite of the risk of persecution and ostracism, and they'll be encouraged by the promise of God's blessings upon those who suffer in his name.

Kids need to know that sharing their faith with others isn't just a religious duty. When God opens kids' hearts to help them see all that he's done for them, sharing their faith with others will be a natural outward expression of their lives as Christians. And their lives will change as they demonstrate their faith through their words and their actions.

For a more comprehensive look at this Core Christian Belief, read Group's ***Get Real: Making Core Christian Beliefs Relevant to Teenagers.***

DEPTHFINDER: HOW THE BIBLE DESCRIBES SHARING FAITH WITH OTHERS

To help you effectively guide your kids toward this Core Christian Belief, use these overviews as a launching point for a more in-depth study of sharing faith.

- **We should be motivated to share our faith with others because of what God has done for us.** Sharing our faith isn't a matter of obligation, but a natural outgrowth of a maturing relationship with God. As we understand more and more what God has done for us and as we realize the fate of those who don't have a personal relationship with him, our natural response is an outpouring of love toward others. Since we have found the greatest treasure in the world, we want those around us to have it, too (Matthew 13:44-45; Luke 15:8-10; Romans 9:1-5; 1 Thessalonians 2:8; and 1 John 4:19).

- **We share our faith through the way we live.** When we become Christians, we automatically become representatives of Christ here on earth. Non-Christians form images of what Christians are and of who our God is based on what they see us do. Therefore, as we seek to obey God, we demonstrate our faith through our lives in these ways:

By demonstrating God's love—God is the source of all love and wants his love to flow through us to others. As we show love for others, we demonstrate that we're truly Jesus' followers (Matthew 25:34-40; Luke 6:31-35; John 13:34-35; Romans 13:9-10; 1 Thessalonians 3:12; and 1 John 4:7-8, 16).

By living a pure life—Jesus lived a pure, honest, sinless life. We're to follow his example by living pure lives, so that no one can question our honesty or integrity. If we keep our lives free from dishonest or immoral actions, people can't legitimately form negative opinions about Christianity because of us. In fact, our honesty and integrity may encourage others to ask why we live the way we do (1 Kings 9:4; 2 Corinthians 8:20-21; Titus 2:2-15; Hebrews 4:15; and 1 Peter 2:11-12; 3:13-16).

- **We share our faith through our words.** Our actions may draw people toward Christ, but only through our words will they be able to understand and accept the gift God offers through Jesus. We need to be able to articulate what Jesus means to us, and we need to be ready to tell others how they, too, can receive God's gift of eternal life. We can verbally share our faith in these ways:

By telling our faith stories—When people become interested in why we're different from the crowd, we need to tell them what Jesus means in our lives. When they hear what Jesus has done for us, they'll be better able to believe in what Jesus can do for them (Luke 8:38-39; John 4:28-29, 39-42; 9:20-27; 1 Timothy 1:12-17; and 1 Peter 3:15).

By telling others about Jesus—This is the heart of sharing our faith. We're to be ready to tell others what Jesus has done in dying as the sacrifice for our sins and how we can have eternal life through him. We cannot, however, convince people to accept God's gift of eternal life. That's the role of the Holy Spirit in their lives (Matthew 28:19-20; John 16:7-11; Acts 1:8; 3:1-26; 4:8-12; 8:1b-4; 16:29-34; 1 Corinthians 2:9-10; 15:1-4; and 1 Thessalonians 1:4-6).

CORE CHRISTIAN BELIEF OVERVIEW

Here are the twenty-four Core Christian Belief categories that form the backbone of Core Belief Bible Study Series:

The Nature of God	Jesus Christ	The Holy Spirit
Humanity	Evil	Suffering
Creation	The Spiritual Realm	The Bible
Salvation	Spiritual Growth	Personal Character
God's Justice	Sin & Forgiveness	The Last Days
Love	The Church	Worship
Authority	Prayer	Family
Service	Relationships	Sharing Faith

Look for Group's Core Belief Bible Study Series books in these other Core Christian Beliefs!

about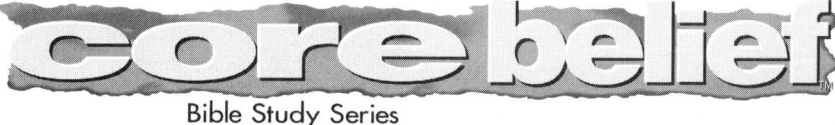
Bible Study Series
for senior high

Think for a moment about your young people. When your students walk out of your youth program after they graduate from junior high or high school, what do you want them to know? What foundation do you want them to have so they can make wise choices?

You probably want them to know the essentials of the Christian faith. You want them to base everything they do on the foundational truths of Christianity. Are you meeting this goal?

If you have any doubt that your kids will walk into adulthood knowing and living by the tenets of the Christian faith, then you've picked up the right book. All the books in Group's Core Belief Bible Study Series encourage young people to discover the essentials of Christianity and to put those essentials into practice. Let us explain...

What Is Group's Core Belief Bible Study Series?

Group's Core Belief Bible Study Series is a biblically in-depth study series for junior high and senior high teenagers. This Bible study series utilizes four defining commitments to create each study. These "plumb lines" provide structure and continuity for every activity, study, project, and discussion. They are:

● **A Commitment to Biblical Depth**—Core Belief Bible Study Series is founded on the belief that kids not only *can* understand the deeper truths of the Bible but also *want* to understand them. Therefore, the activities and studies in this series strive to explain the "why" behind every truth we explore. That way, kids learn principles, not just rules.

● **A Commitment to Relevance**—Most kids aren't interested in abstract theories or doctrines about the universe. They want to know how to live successfully right now, today, in the heat of problems they can't ignore. Because of this, each study connects a real-life need with biblical principles that speak directly to that need. This study series finally bridges the gap between Bible truths and the real-world issues kids face.

● **A Commitment to Variety**—Today's young people have been raised in a sound bite world. They demand variety. For that reason, no two meetings in this study series are shaped exactly the same.

● **A Commitment to Active and Interactive Learning**—Active learning is learning by doing. Interactive learning simply takes active learning a step further by having kids teach each other what they've learned. It's a process that helps kids internalize and remember their discoveries.

For a more detailed description of these concepts, see the section titled "Why Active and Interactive Learning Works With Teenagers" beginning on page 57.

So how can you accomplish all this in a set of four easy-to-lead Bible studies? By weaving together various "power" elements to produce a fun experience that leaves kids challenged and encouraged.

- **A Relevant Topic**—More than ever before, kids live in the now. What matters to them and what attracts their hearts is what's happening in their world at this moment. For this reason, every Core Belief Bible Study focuses on a particular hot topic that kids care about.

- **A Core Christian Belief**—Group's Core Belief Bible Study Series organizes the wealth of Christian truth and experience into twenty-four Core Christian Belief categories. These twenty-four headings act as umbrellas for a collection of detailed beliefs that define Christianity and set it apart from the world and every other religion. Each book in this series features one Core Christian Belief with lessons suited for junior high or senior high students.

  "But," you ask, "won't my kids be bored talking about all these spiritual beliefs?" No way! As a youth leader, you know the value of using hot topics to connect with young people. Ultimately teenagers talk about issues because they're searching for meaning in their lives. They want to find the one equation that will make sense of all the confusing events happening around them. Each Core Belief Bible Study answers that need by connecting a hot topic with a powerful Christian principle. Kids walk away from the study with something more solid than just the shifting ebb and flow of their own opinions. They walk away with a deeper understanding of their Christian faith.

- **The Point**—This simple statement is designed to be the intersection between the Core Christian Belief and the hot topic. Everything in the study ultimately focuses on The Point so that kids study it and allow it time to sink into their hearts.

- **The Study at a Glance**—A quick look at this chart will tell you what kids will do, how long it will take them to do it, and what supplies you'll need to get it done.

- **The Bible Connection**—This is the power base of each study. Whether it's just one verse or several chapters, The Bible Connection provides the vital link between kids' minds and their hearts. The content of each Core Belief Bible Study reflects the belief that the true power of God—the power to expose, heal, and change kids' lives—is contained in his Word.

- **Depthfinder Boxes**—These informative sidelights located throughout each study add insight into a particular passage, word, historical fact, or Christian doctrine. Depthfinder boxes also provide insight into teen culture, adolescent development, current events, and philosophy.

- **Leader Tips**—These handy information boxes coach you through the study, offering helpful suggestions on everything from altering activities for different-sized groups to streamlining discussions to using effective discipline techniques.

- **Handouts**—Most Core Belief Bible Studies include photocopiable handouts to use with your group. Handouts might take the form of a fun game, a lively discussion starter, or a challenging study page for kids to take home—anything to make your study more meaningful and effective.

Helpful Stuff   12

The Last Word on Core Belief Bible Studies

Soon after you begin to use Group's Core Belief Bible Study Series, you'll see signs of real growth in your group members. Your kids will gain a deeper understanding of the Bible and of their own Christian faith. They'll see more clearly how a relationship with Jesus affects their daily lives. And they'll grow closer to God.

But that's not all. You'll also see kids grow closer to one another.

That's because this series is founded on the principle that Christian faith grows best in the context of relationship. Each study uses a variety of interactive pairs and small groups and always includes discussion questions that promote deeper relationships. The friendships kids will build through this study series will enable them to grow *together* toward a deeper relationship with God.

THE ISSUE: Sharing Faith

How to Talk with Others About God

BY RICK LAWRENCE

■ Let's say a visitor walks into your youth meeting, but instead of a normal greeting like "What's up?" or "How's it goin'?" he says, "What's your story? Why are you really here?" ■ What would your group members say? Do they have stories to tell about their relationships with God? And if they do, do they know how to tell them? ■ What if one of your group members spoke out and said, "My story is about grace—how much I've needed it and how often God has offered it to me. My story is about trying to make life work on my own, but ending up lost, isolated, lonely, and afraid. And my story is about how, in the middle of that darkness, God loved me and offered to be the co-author of my life. Now I'm learning that God doesn't want to write my story for me—he wants to write it with me. And as we create together, I'm learning that my story can actually offer hope and truth to others. That's my story. Would you like to hear more?" ■ Your teenagers each have a story to tell—one that God has helped write. Others need to hear those stories—people who need hope but can't find it. This study will help your kids find God's grace in their stories, then tell their stories to those around them.

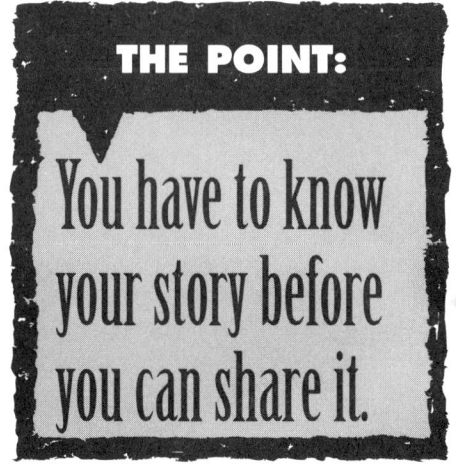

THE POINT:

You have to know your story before you can share it.

The Study AT A GLANCE

SECTION	MINUTES	WHAT STUDENTS WILL DO	SUPPLIES
Room Transformation	10 to 15	SPLATTERED STORIES—Create a personalized space on the floor and then share something about themselves.	Newsprint, tape, pens, colored markers, old magazines, glue, scissors
Personal Investigation	15 to 20	TELL ME A STORY—Tell stories from real life and journal how others' stories impact them.	Pens, markers
Bible Investigation	15 to 20	A TALE OF TWO MEN—Explore the lives of two men in the Bible whose stories were powerfully impacted by God.	Newsprint, tape, markers, Bibles
Creative Giving Experience	5 to 10	GIVE YOUR LIFE AWAY—Create personal symbols that represent God's impact on their stories and then choose ways to use the symbols in telling their stories.	Markers, pens

notes:

THE POINT OF "HOW TO TALK WITH OTHERS ABOUT GOD":

You have to know your story before you can share it.

THE BIBLE CONNECTION

2 KINGS 22:1–23:30 — King Josiah reminds God's people of God's role in their story.

PHILIPPIANS 3:2-11 — Paul tells how God "rewrote" his life's story—saving him from pride and giving him new life.

In this study, kids will explore the impact God has had on their personal stories, the personal stories of others in your group, and the stories of two Bible characters.

By discovering God's role as a co-author of their personal stories, kids will learn how to share those stories with others in practical, natural ways.

Explore the verses in The Bible Connection, then examine the information in the Depthfinder boxes throughout the study to gain a deeper understanding of how these Scriptures connect with your young people.

BEFORE THE STUDY

Move the furniture to the sides of your meeting room and cover the floor with newsprint (you may want to tape the newsprint to the floor in spots to keep it from shifting). Gather old magazines, markers, pens, glue, and scissors, and pile them together in the center of the room.

LEADER TIP for The Study

Whenever groups discuss a list of questions, write the questions on newsprint and tape the newsprint to the wall so groups can discuss the questions at their own pace.

THE STUDY

LEADER TIP for The Study

What about kids who say they're Christians but have no evident relationship with Christ? If kids claim God has no impact on their lives, consider calling them aside and lovingly confronting them with these difficult questions:
- What does being a Christian mean to you?
- The Bible teaches that being a Christian means receiving God's forgiveness for our sins, then following Jesus every day. Do you think this is true? Why or why not?
- If what the Bible teaches is true, why would it be important for a follower of Jesus to have an ongoing, daily relationship with him?
- Do you want an ongoing, daily relationship with Jesus? Why or why not?

If kids express interest in a personal relationship with Jesus, pray with them right there, asking God to guide them into a personal relationship with him.

ROOM TRANSFORMATION ▼

Splattered Stories (10 to 15 minutes) As teenagers enter your meeting room, have them remove their shoes. Then have kids spread out around the room and each create his or her own "personal space" on the floor by drawing a shape (a circle, square, letter outline, or whatever) on the newsprint. The shape should be big enough to sit in. Ask kids to decorate their shapes however they'd like (point them to the supply pile for decoration ideas).

When kids finish, form groups of three by having kids get together with two other people whose shapes are located close to theirs. Have trios draw a circle in the space between their three shapes, then sit down around the circle.

Say: **Show your two partners your personal space design, then draw a pathway from your shape to the circle you just created.**

Once trios finish this task, say: **Now complete the following statement about each of your partners by writing inside the pathway that leads from your personal space to the circle. Here's the statement: "[Name], based on how you've decorated your personal space, I think you're a person who..."**

When trios are finished, say: **Now, look at what your group members wrote about you. Tell them whether they're right or wrong about you and why.**

After a few minutes, ask kids to tell what they learned about their group members. Then ask:
- **How did it feel to have others draw conclusions about you with very little information?**
- **How did it feel when they were right? wrong?**
- **How did you feel when you gave someone in your group feedback and that person disagreed with your conclusions? agreed?**
- **How are all these feelings like the way you feel when you're relating with people at school, home, work, or church?**

Say: **Tell your partners something you'd like them to know about you. When you're finished, write in the circle one thing you liked about what your partners shared.**

Then say: **Each of us has a story to tell about who we are. Often the people around us, even our closest friends, don't understand us because we're not always that good at telling our own stories. Today we'll investigate our own stories and the stories of the people around us and learn how we can help others by sharing God's impact on our lives. Remember this: <u>You have to know your story before you can share it with others.</u>**

How to Talk With Others About God 18

PERSONAL INVESTIGATION ▼

Tell Me a Story
(15 to 20 minutes)

Ask kids to find a new partner—someone not in their trio. Have pairs draw a pathway between their personal spaces. Then say: **The next experience will be more personal. Inside your personal space, write a short story about God's influence in your life. For example, you could write about a time when...**

● **things seemed bleak, but God somehow gave you hope.**
● **you were hurt and confused because God didn't act the way you expected him to.**
● **you felt close to God.**
● **you felt far away from God.**
● **you felt like standing up for God.**
● **you felt like you really needed God in your life.**

After a few minutes, say: **Now I'd like you to talk to your partner about what you wrote. Be sure you tell your partner something you learned about yourself because of this life experience.**

After partners share, have them discuss these questions:

● **Was it easy to think of some way God has impacted your story? Why or why not?**
● **What's most difficult about telling someone else about God's impact on your life?**
● **If your school friends knew about God's impact on you, how would that affect them?**
● **What does it mean to share your faith with someone?**

Say: **Even though God has co-authored our stories, it's easy to "edit out" his impact on us when we're telling our stories to others. That's why it's important to be prepared to talk with others about God's role in our lives. You have to know your story before you can share it. To discover more about how to do this, let's explore how God deeply impacted the stories of two men and what happened because of his impact.**

DEPTHFINDER — UNDERSTANDING THESE KIDS

How do teenagers respond to journaling? Well, high school teacher Nancy Rubin has used journaling as an integral part of her Social Living class for years. She has had her students journal about topics such as sex, family life, abuse, and abortion. In her book *Ask Me If I Care*, she writes,

"Whenever I read [aloud] from the journals, I could always sense a different atmosphere in the room and an involvement that was rarely there at other times. Some students found relief in discovering that they were not alone with their problems, or that, by comparison, their problems were not as bad as they originally thought. Others became more sensitive to the burdens that their classmates carry. I found this method of sharing ideas [stories] to be a powerful approach to teaching, and the students' writings very quickly became an integral part of my course."

How to Talk With Others About God

BIBLE INVESTIGATION ▼

A Tale of Two Men

(15 to 20 minutes) At opposite ends of your meeting area, draw circles on the newsprint and write in one the name Paul and in the other the name Josiah. Then say: **Imagine that marriage and a family will one day be a part of your story. Imagine that you and your spouse are pregnant with a son, and you have just these two names to choose from—which one would you pick to name your son? Once you decide, draw a pathway to the circle that represents your choice and sit near it.**

Once kids have gathered by the two circles, give each group a Bible and ask each group to pick a reader. Then say: **In a moment I'll assign each reader a Bible passage to read aloud. As you listen to the passage, think about how you'd answer these two questions: "How did God impact this person's story?" and "Why did this person respond to God the way he did?"**

Tell the Josiah group reader to read aloud 2 Kings 22:1–23:30. Have the Paul group reader read aloud Philippians 3:2-11. While the readers are reading, write the two questions on newsprint and tape the newsprint to the wall.

When both readers finish, have groups discuss the two questions you wrote on the newsprint. Then have each group appoint a reporter to tell what the group learned about its biblical character. After the reporters share, say: **I'd like to add one more story to those we've been studying—it's my story.**

DEPTH FINDER — UNDERSTANDING THE BIBLE

Josiah stands out in Old Testament history as a passionate reformer and humble leader who, as king of Judah, tried to lead his people into repentance for their idol worship and cavalier attitude toward God.

Josiah began his journey as a leader when he was only eight years old. Before he became king, Judah had grown corrupt with foreign, idolatrous influences. For more than fifty years, idol worship had replaced the law of Moses and immorality was rampant. In fact, the people of Judah so ignored God in their daily lives that Josiah didn't even know what God expected of his people. When workers restoring the temple in Jerusalem discovered a copy of God's laws, Josiah read them and grieved that the people had strayed so far from God's design for them.

When Josiah was just sixteen, he stopped practicing the traditional idol worship of the people and searched for ways to honor God in his life. Then when he was twenty, he decided to vigorously purge idolatry from Judah. He ordered altars, statues, and icons of pagan gods destroyed. He banished prostitutes from the temple, banned child sacrifices, and removed idolatrous religious leaders from office. At the same time, he repopularized the reading of God's laws and personally pledged to follow them with all his heart.

When he was thirty-nine, Josiah was killed in battle fighting the Egyptians. And soon after, Judah returned to idol worship.

Tell your group members your own story of how God has changed your life. Then call everyone together and ask:

● **How have these stories—mine, Josiah's, and Paul's—impacted you?**

● **What does that say about how your story can impact others for Christ?**

Have kids look around the room at the newsprint "network" they've created. Ask:

● **How is creating these pathways on the newsprint like sharing our stories with others in real life?**

● **What would happen to you if you never shared your story with anyone?**

Say: **You have to know your story before you can share it**. Now let's learn more about ways you can share your story with others.

CREATIVE GIVING EXPERIENCE ▼

Give Your Life Away (5 to 10 minutes)

Say: **We've begun to see God's impact on others' stories and our own. But how can we let others know the good news that God loves us and wants to be a co-author with us in creating our life stories? In your personal space, I'd like you to create a symbol or drawing that represents God's impact on your life's story. Then we'll discuss ways you can use your symbol or drawing to tell your story. But before we begin, let's ask our "co-author" to help us share our stories with the people around us.**

Open the prayer time by asking God to show kids how he has impacted their lives, then invite kids to express their own prayers to God, either silently or aloud.

After the prayer time, pile colored markers in the center of your room for kids to use in creating their symbols. When kids finish, have two or three young people explain their symbols' meanings to the group.

Then say: **To close, I'd like each of you to tear your symbol out of your personal space, then write on the back one way you can use your symbol to tell others about God's impact on your life. For example, you could draw your symbol on all your school notebooks, then use it as an opportunity to share your story with friends at school.**

When kids are finished, say: **I challenge you to follow through with your idea this week. Now that you know something of your story, you can share it with others!**

How to Talk With Others About God 21

THE ISSUE: Joy

THE JOY OF THE LORD IS MY STRENGTH

Exploring and Sharing Joy as Christians

by Jane Vogel

■ Pop quiz: Who would you rather be like, Tigger or Eeyore? ■ OK, if that's too simplistic, think of this: Who was more attractive to the public: Princess Diana or Prince Charles? ■ As the many outpourings of emotion over the princess's death made clear, the charm of "the people's princess" lay in more than her physical beauty and her glamorous lifestyle. Diana won hearts by her obvious love of life, even when life was handing her lemons. She had an inner glow that drew people as a candle draws moths to its light. ■ If Diana's inner joy could have that effect on people, think what an impact the real thing could make! Think what an attraction the joy of the Lord would have if people were only able to see it clearly in our lives! ■ Use this lesson to help kids see that they don't always have to *do* something to share their faith; sometimes the way they live their lives is the strongest witness. Help kids discover that when non-Christians see the amazing life transformations that come when people live lives of true joy in Christ, they will want to find out how they can live their lives the same way. ■ Equip your students to be more than just "a candle in the wind"; challenge them to be the light of the world.

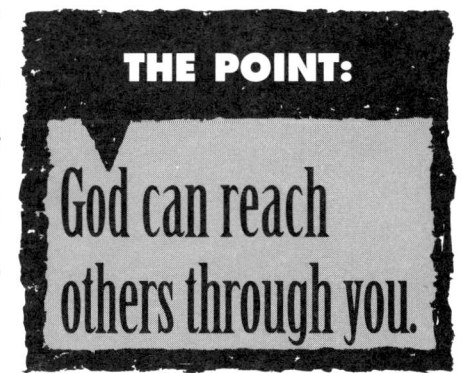

THE POINT:

God can reach others through you.

The Study AT A GLANCE

SECTION	MINUTES	WHAT STUDENTS WILL DO	SUPPLIES
Getting Focused	15 to 20	THERE AIN'T NOTHIN' LIKE THE REAL THING, BABY—Do a taste test to see if they can tell the real thing from the imitation, then discuss the difference between expressing true joy and just faking it.	Bibles, samples of food and beverages, scissors, paper, pens, "ballot" boxes or bags, markers, white board or newsprint
Digging Deeper	20 to 25	DRAWN TO THE LIGHT—Make life-size examples of joyful and crabby Christians, then reflect on how well they exhibit true joy.	Bibles, long sheets of newsprint, markers, magazines, scissors, glue sticks, definitions and qualities of joy from the previous activity
Making It Practical	10 to 15	GETTING DOWN TO BUSINESS—Make magnetized business cards to remind them of practical ways to demonstrate the joy of the Lord.	Bible, paper, markers, newsprint, scissors, and self-adhesive business-card-sized magnets

notes:

THE POINT OF "THE JOY OF THE LORD IS MY STRENGTH":

God can reach others through you.

THE BIBLE CONNECTION

MATTHEW 5:13-16 — The expression of Christ in our lives can make our faith attractive to other people.

1 PETER 1:3-9 — Through Christ, we have a joy that cannot be explained even when circumstances make us sad.

In this study, kids will examine the Bible's definition of true joy and contrast it both with the world's view of happiness and with the negative image people sometimes have of the Christian life. They'll evaluate how well they exhibit the joy of the Lord and write specific ways they can express the joy they have in Jesus.

Through these explorations, kids will discover that true joy can draw others to Jesus, the source of that joy. They'll be affirmed that, through their expressions of joy, God can use them to reach others.

Explore the verses in The Bible Connection, then examine the information in the Depthfinder boxes throughout the study to gain a deeper understanding of how these Scriptures connect with your young people.

BEFORE THE STUDY

Before the meeting, set up one or more taste tests—set out food or beverage samples in pairs, with each pair consisting of the real thing and an imitation (for example, you might use a name brand cola and a generic cola, real chocolate chips and chocolate-flavored baking morsels, and real ice cream and frozen nondairy dessert). Remove all labels that would indicate which sample is the real thing and which is the imitation. Label each sample in a pair either "A" or "B" (making sure that in some pairs the imitation is A and in some it is B so that kids don't find a pattern), and provide pens and slips of paper for kids to use as ballots. Place a box or a paper bag by each pair of samples for kids to put their completed ballots in.

You'll need self-adhesive business-card-sized magnets for the "Getting Down to Business" activity. These are available at office supply stores; they're made for business people to attach to their business cards.

LEADER TIP for The Study

Because this topic can be so powerful and relevant to kids' lives, your group members may be tempted to get caught up in issues and lose sight of the deeper biblical principle found in The Point. Help your kids grasp The Point by guiding kids to focus on the biblical investigation and discussing how God's truth connects with reality in their lives.

The Joy of the Lord Is My Strength

THE STUDY

GETTING FOCUSED ▼

There Ain't Nothin' Like the Real Thing, Baby (15 to 20 minutes)

As kids arrive, conduct a taste test by letting kids taste the samples you set out before the study. For each pair of samples, instruct kids to write the letter of the sample that they think is the real thing on a slip of paper and put it in the ballot box or bag by that pair of samples.

When everyone has had a chance to sample and vote, unveil the identities of the samples and see whether the kids were able to tell the difference. (For the discussion that follows, it doesn't matter whether kids guessed right or wrong.) Ask:

● **How could you tell the real thing from the imitation?**
● **Why do the imitations want to pass themselves off as the real thing?**
● **Today we're going to talk about Christian joy. Can you think of ways people try to fake joy? Explain.**
● **How might you be able to tell fake joy from the real thing?**

Say: **We talk a lot about joy. Let's take a better look at what true joy really is.**

Form groups of four. Hand out Bibles, paper, and pens.

Say: **In your foursome, read 1 Peter 1:3-9 and write a definition of true joy based on that passage.**

As foursomes finish their definitions, say: **Stay in your group of**

> **LEADER TIP**
> for There Ain't Nothin' Like the Real Thing, Baby
>
> As kids share stories about people who show true joy in their lives, they may not know exactly why they have chosen those people as examples. You can help deepen their understanding by identifying *actions* (these may be things such as listening to others; expressing faith or thankfulness, even in a crisis; smiling a lot; or tackling tough jobs with energy and enthusiasm) and *attitudes* (these may be things such as a positive outlook, inner peace, or confidence) that kids mention in their descriptions of joyful people they know.

> **LEADER TIP**
> for There Ain't Nothin' Like the Real Thing, Baby
>
> If you think kids may have difficulty thinking of examples, be ready with an example of your own that you can share.

DEPTH FINDER — NO COP-OUTS

It's tempting—perhaps especially for self-conscious teenagers who don't want to risk embarrassing themselves—to limit our faith sharing to the nonverbal. It's easy to rationalize that if actions speak louder than words, we don't really ever have to say the words.

God, of course, doesn't see it quite this way. Scripture makes it clear that Christians are to share their faith through both word and action. Certainly our lifestyles are to be joyful as they demonstrate what Lord we serve. But we are also to be salt and light (as this passage in Matthew reminds us) in what we say. Colossians 4:3-6 uses the same salt imagery that we see in Matthew (see the New International Version), but here it is very clear that being salt includes speaking the gospel to unbelievers: "Make the most of your chances to tell others the Good News" (Colossians 4:5a, The Living Bible).

The verbal and nonverbal sharing of our faith go hand in hand. The joy that people see in our lives backs up the words we speak.

The Joy of the Lord Is My Strength

> ### DEPTHFINDER — UNDERSTANDING THE BIBLE
>
> Christian joy is more than just feeling happy. Happiness is usually a response to external circumstances: getting good grades on final exams, enjoying an evening out with friends, or having a "good hair day." True joy, however, goes deeper than circumstances. As 1 Peter 1:3-5 shows, Christian joy is founded on the reality of our new life in Christ, our status as members of God's own family, and our hope that stretches beyond the present into eternity. This is not to say that joy is reserved for some distant time in the sweet by-and-by, however; because of our love and our faith now, we can also experience deep joy now (see 1 Peter 1:8), even when external circumstances are unpleasant.

LEADER TIP for The Study

Whenever groups discuss a list of questions, write the questions on newsprint and tape the newsprint to the wall so groups can discuss the questions at their own pace.

four, and think about people you know who are truly joyful Christians. Then have each person in your group tell the rest of the foursome about specific ways someone you know exhibited true joy.

After a few minutes, have each foursome share its definition of joy with the whole group and then share one or more of the "true joy" stories. As kids share their ideas, write the definitions on a white board or a sheet of newsprint. Listen for qualities in the people described, and write those down as well.

When every foursome has had a chance to report, ask:
- **What do you see as the relationship between suffering and joy?**
- **When is it hard for you to be joyful?**
- **How is it that some people can be joyful even in hard times?**
- **What impact do you think joy has on others—for example, how could your joy affect people who see your joy even in hard times?**
- **How might your joy enable <u>God to reach others through you</u>?**

DIGGING DEEPER ▼

Drawn to the Light (20 to 25 minutes)

Have kids stay in their same groups of four. Give foursomes long sheets of newsprint, magazines, scissors, markers, and glue sticks. Assign half of the groups to make life-size "Joyful Christians" and the other half to make "Crabby Christians." Suggest each group trace a person on the paper, cut out various features from magazines, and add its own artwork.

Say: **The figure you create should be more than just a smiling or a frowning person; it should include things representative of positive or negative attitudes associated with Christians. For example, Crabby Christian might have a speech balloon around magazine pictures of a happy couple and a sports car—both crossed out. Next to the pictures inside the speech balloon might**

The Joy of the Lord Is My Strength   **27**

be the words, "Thou shalt not engage in public displays of affection" and "Thou shalt not drive fast cars."

After foursomes have made their figures, let them display and explain them. Then have kids read Matthew 5:14-16 in their foursomes and discuss these questions:

● **How is a joyful Christian like a city on a hill?**

● **What are some of the things about a joyful Christian that make his or her faith attractive to others?**

● **Who do you know who is a joyful Christian? How does that person's joy show?**

● **Do you consider yourself a joyful Christian?**

Refer to the definitions of joy and the qualities of a joyful Christian that you compiled in the previous activity as kids reflect on whether their lives demonstrate true joy.

Have kids form pairs. Say: **Share with your partner one area in your life in which you want to develop or show more joy. For example, you might want to become more joyful in your relationships with your family, or you might want to be able to find more joy in your role as a student. After you've each shared those areas, don't tell your partner what he or she ought to do to be more joyful! Instead of giving advice, spend a few minutes praying for your partner and the area he or she shared.**

Say: <u>God can reach others through you.</u> **In fact, he probably already does. Share with your partner one way that you see the joy of the Lord in his or her life. Be as specific**

DEPTH FINDER — THE DEPRESSED TEENAGER

While every teenager feels blue once in a while, and even the strongest Christians can think of situations that challenge their capacity for joy, those who suffer from depression may find the whole concept of joy completely alien.

If a teenager you know is suffering from depression, you may see one or more of these warning signs:

● a loss of interest in life;
● decreased interest in usual activities;
● a change in eating habits (either loss of appetite or compulsive eating);
● sleep disturbances;
● loss of energy;
● withdrawal from others;
● feelings of alienation, worthlessness, hopelessness, and guilt;
● an inability to concentrate; or
● suicidal thoughts or actions.

(taken from William J. Rowley, *Equipped to Care*)

For such teenagers, the idea that Christians are called to joy can lead not to a renewed and joyful life, but to a sense of guilt. If you fear that one of your students suffers from depression, refer that student (and his or her parents) to professional counseling.

DEPTH FINDER: POSITIVES VS. PROHIBITIONS

When you debrief the "Drawn to the Light" activity, address ways we as Christians can look at things we ought not do—such as engaging in drunkenness or sexual promiscuity—in a positive light. For example, you might point out that we don't need alcohol to have fun or that we don't need to barter our bodies to feel accepted. Let kids know two things: (1) We should never sacrifice moral standards just because we think it will make us more appealing as we share our faith with others; and (2) we do not need to present the challenges of the Christian life in a negative light. We can take a stand on moral issues without being Crabby Christians.

as you can. For example, your partner might be someone who tries to have a smile for everyone. That's one way of reaching out. Or maybe you've seen your partner deal with a disappointment or an inconvenience without losing his or her cool. That's evidence of Christian joy.

"For God, who said, 'Let light shine out of the darkness,' made his light shine in our hearts to give us the light of the knowledge of the glory of God in the face of Christ."

—2 Corinthians 4:6

MAKING IT PRACTICAL ▼

Getting Down to Business (10 to 15 minutes) Read Matthew 5:14-16 aloud again, and say: **God can reach others through you.** Often when we think about reaching others for God, we think about saying the right things. And it's important to be able to talk about our faith. But did you notice that this passage doesn't talk at all about what we say, just about what we do? Ask:

● **What are some things you could do to show your joy?**

● **How might those actions make your faith attractive to other people?**

● **How do you feel about the idea that your attitudes and actions can be as important a part of your faith sharing as what you say?**

Hand out self-adhesive business-card-sized magnets, paper, and markers. Say: **It's our business as Christians to live as lights—**

"**Shout for joy** to the Lord, all the earth. Worship the Lord with gladness; come before him with joyful songs. Know that the Lord is God. It is he who made us, and we are his; we are his people, the sheep of his pasture. Enter his gates with thanksgiving and his courts with praise; give thanks to him and praise his name. For the Lord is good and his love endures forever; his faithfulness continues through all generations."

—Psalm 100

DEPTHFINDER: OUTREACH EVENTS

A terrific way for your group members to let God use them to reach others is by hosting an event for their non-Christian friends. This event can be as simple or as involved as your resources permit, but it should include certain things:

• It should be fun. While fun is not the same as joy, it certainly helps non-Christians see that the Christian life is not all gloom and doom!

• It should be nonthreatening. Using church jargon, expecting kids to know where to look in the Bible or song book, and even telling kids to meet in the narthex can all be intimidating to those who don't have much experience with church life.

• It should include a clear presentation of the gospel. After all, it isn't outreach if you don't reach out, is it? Such a presentation need not be long or heavy-handed, and you don't have to call for a public commitment; but you do need to be sure that the kids who come have a chance to discover the source of true joy!

people whose joy makes the Christian faith attractive. Ask:

● **What are some specific ways we could show our joy this week?**

Compile a list of ideas on newsprint, then have each person choose one idea to implement this week. Have kids each make a "business card" with an idea, a logo, or a slogan reminding them of the idea. Have kids attach their business cards to the magnets, and urge them to stick their magnets in their school lockers where they'll see them and be reminded every day.

Close the meeting with this reminder: **God can reach others through you! Let your light shine so that others will be drawn to Jesus, the light of the world.**

THE ISSUE: Global Missions

The World Is My Church
Love in Action

BY PAMELA J. SHOUP

■ "Good morning, Mr. Phelps. Your mission, should you choose to accept it..." Familiar words from the old *Mission: Impossible* TV show could apply to mission work for youth today. Of course, on TV the mission message self-destructed in a few seconds. But the message of eternal life through Christ is indestructible. ■ Today hundreds of thousands of missionaries have received the call to work around the globe to spread the message of the gospel to non-Christians. And billions still need to be reached by the message. Mission work is a selfless job that often requires hardship, suffering, and sometimes even death. Not an attractive-sounding career choice for a teenager. ■ But teenagers' youthful idealism—a desire to change the world (in a few weeks or less)—gives them a natural affinity toward mission work. Get kids involved in missions close to home or across the world to help them experience true Christian fellowship and many will have life-changing experiences. Every person may not feel the call to enter international missions and share Christ with people in the deepest, darkest parts of Africa or the Muslim-dominated Middle East. But everyone has a place where he or she can share Christ—with friends and in his or her own community, where the need may be as great as somewhere across an ocean. ■ The power to share Christ comes from the Holy Spirit as Jesus told his disciples in Acts 1:8a: "You will receive power when the Holy Spirit comes on you; and you will be my witnesses." Through this study your teenagers will have the opportunity to explore missions; identify their own call to share their faith; and ask themselves, "What can I do to bring Christ's message to the world?" Mission: Possible!

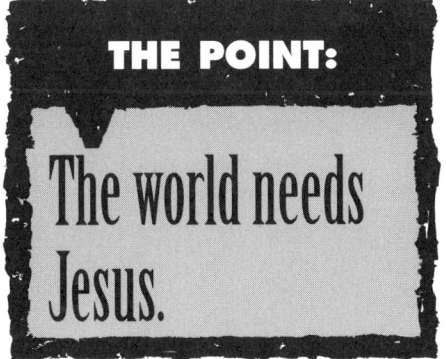

THE POINT:
The world needs Jesus.

The Study
AT A GLANCE

SECTION	MINUTES	WHAT STUDENTS WILL DO	SUPPLIES
Opener	5 to 10	FISHERS OF MEN—Explore the idea of being called to mission work.	Bible, paper, scissors, pen
Active Experience	5 to 10	CAST THE NET—Create fictional countries and identify missionary needs.	Bibles, poster board, markers
	20 to 25	TRUE STORIES—Share real-life stories of missionaries, pray for unreached people, and identify how they can support foreign missions.	"Living the Faith" handout (pp. 44-45), scissors, newsprint, markers, globe or map of the world, tape, pushpins
Reflection and Commitment	up to 10	COMFORT ZONES—Identify local mission needs and be challenged to reach outside their comfort zones.	Newsprint, marker, tape, list of ways to support foreign missions from "True Stories" activity
	up to 10	POWER FROM THE SPIRIT—Reflect on their own calls to missions and commit to service.	Bibles, candles, matches, journals or paper, pens

notes:

THE POINT OF "THE WORLD IS MY CHURCH":
The world needs Jesus.

THE BIBLE CONNECTION

MATTHEW 25:31-46	Jesus teaches about those who will inherit the kingdom of heaven.
MATTHEW 28:18-20	Christ appears to his eleven disciples and instructs them to make disciples of all nations.
MARK 1:17	As Jesus calls his disciples, he promises to make them "fishers of men."
ACTS 1:8	The resurrected Christ promises the apostles they will receive power to share faith when the Holy Spirit comes upon them.
EPHESIANS 6:19	Paul prays for the gift of words to help him spread the gospel fearlessly.

In this study, kids will learn about God's call to people to enter his service, and they will identify and explore missionary needs globally as well as in their own communities.

By doing this, kids will explore the power of the Holy Spirit in sharing their faith and make a commitment to share their faith through a mission project.

Explore the verses in The Bible Connection, then examine the information in the Depthfinder boxes throughout the study to gain a deeper understanding of how these Scriptures connect with your young people.

BEFORE THE STUDY

Before the study, prepare four "mission slips" on different slips of paper for the "Fishers of Men" activity. The four different slips should read, "living in a foreign country"; "performing, singing, or acting"; "teaching or practicing medicine"; and "bringing people to Christ."

For the "True Stories" activity, hang a map of the world in your meeting room (or bring in a globe).

LEADER TIP for The Study

Because this topic can be so powerful and relevant to kids' lives, your group members may be tempted to get caught up in issues and lose sight of the deeper biblical principle found in The Point. Help your kids grasp The Point by guiding kids to focus on the biblical investigation and discussing how God's truth connects with reality in their lives.

THE STUDY

OPENER ▼

Fishers of Men (5 to 10 minutes)

LEADER TIP for Fishers of Men

You may adjust the number of volunteers according to the size of your group. (Plan on one volunteer for every four students.) Reduce or expand the number of mission slips as needed. You might choose students who are natural leaders so each leader will attract at least one follower.

As teenagers arrive, choose four volunteers, take them aside, and tell them that the goal in the opening activity is for each of them to get the most people to join his or her group. Have each volunteer choose one of the mission slips you prepared before the study. Explain that volunteers are to entice other students to join their groups based on the students' interests and the leader's persuasiveness. For example, leaders might promote the benefits of joining their groups by telling about the excitement of living overseas, opportunities to use various talents, a life dedicated to helping others, or a life dedicated to spreading God's Word.

Once everyone has arrived, welcome teenagers and say: **Let's start off today with an activity to get everybody up and moving around. I've selected four people who each have a mission to accomplish. Listen to what they have to say, and decide which mission you would like to be a part of.**

Allow about a minute for groups to form, then have kids sit down with their groups. If any leader was unable to attract followers, have him or her sit with another group. Ask:

● **Leaders, how did you get people to join your group?**
● **Followers, why did you choose the area of need that you chose?**
● **Leaders, why couldn't some of you get many followers?**
● **Followers, did your leader offer promises he or she couldn't fulfill? Explain.**
● **Does God ever offer promises he can't fulfill? Explain.**

Say: **I call this activity "Fishers of Men," based on Mark 1:17, since you all "fished" for followers for your missions.** Have a volunteer read Mark 1:17 aloud, and say: **Modern-day fishers of men are missionaries, and today we're going to explore mission work at home and throughout the world because the world needs Jesus. The message spread by missions is God's truth. God is always true to his promises and his Word, and that's what we as Christians need to tell the world.**

LEADER TIP for The Study

Whenever groups discuss a list of questions, write the questions on newsprint and tape the newsprint to the wall so groups can discuss the questions at their own pace.

The disciples received a "call" from Jesus to become his followers. Today you'll have a chance to explore your own thoughts and feelings about mission work and perhaps determine whether God might want you to serve him in that way. Have kids discuss the following questions in their groups:

● **How might you know if God wants you to do mission work?**
● **How might you determine an area of need that you could meet?**

The World Is My Church 36

● **What various talents, knowledge, or education would be helpful in mission work?**

Allow groups to share some of their answers, then say: **Singing and performing, traveling to foreign countries, spreading the Word of God, or teaching and doing medical work are some of the jobs done by missionaries as they use the truth of God's Word to gather followers for Jesus. Let's take a closer look at mission work.**

ACTIVE EXPERIENCE ▼

Cast the Net (5 to 10 minutes)

Have kids divide into groups of four to six (or remain in their groups from the previous activity), and have members of each group sit together on the floor. Give each group a sheet of poster board, a marker, and a Bible.

Say: **On your poster board, draw a shape of a fictional country. Make up a name and a fictional religion for your country, and write them on the poster board.**

Give kids a few minutes to complete the task, then say: **Now you are missionaries who are going to bring Christianity to this country because <u>the world needs Jesus</u>. On your poster board, list the needs the people in your country might have that missionaries could respond to. I'll come around and give you some ideas if you need help.**

After a few minutes, have each group share its poster with the entire group. They may elaborate on any interesting "facts" about their country, its religion, or its mission needs. Then have each group read Matthew 25:31-46 together and discuss these questions:

● **How do your lists of mission needs correspond with the directives Jesus gave in this Scripture passage?**

● **How can you as a missionary share your faith in all that you do?**

● **When you as a missionary serve others, who are you really serving? Explain.**

Say: **You've come up with some real needs for your fictional countries. When you serve God's people, you are serving God. You can meet <u>the world's need for Jesus</u>. Now let's look at some real-life missionary stories in real countries.**

True Stories (20 to 25 minutes)

Have kids divide into four groups, and distribute a different portion of the "Living the Faith" handout (pp. 44-45) to each group.

Have groups read their stories and then take turns teaching the stories to the other groups in creative ways. For example, they may act out the stories, draw the stories, or do dramatic readings of the stories. After kids have shared their stories, have them find the countries described on the globe or world map. (Kids can place pushpins on the map, if you'd like.)

LEADER TIP for Cast the Net

If any groups are struggling for ideas, give them some of these suggestions: building churches or houses, establishing schools, starting Bible studies, training native missionaries and pastors, building water systems, responding to medical and health needs, easing suffering caused by war or natural disasters, translating or interpreting the local language, providing Bibles in native languages, or bringing people to Christ through music and drama as well as through one-on-one sharing of the gospel of Christ.

LEADER TIP for True Stories

If you have a small group, only use as many stories as you need. (A group may be one or two people.)

LEADER TIP for True Stories

If you use a world map and pushpins to mark locations of missionaries, make sure you know where these countries are before the study so you can help kids find them if necessary. Also, you might make it an ongoing project to mark locations of missionaries you correspond with, countries that might be part of your own students' mission commitments, and locations of any missionaries your church sponsors.

LEADER TIP for True Stories

If you want more information on other unreached people groups to share with your group, contact AD2000 and Beyond Movement, 2860 S. Circle Dr., Ste. 2112, Colorado Springs, CO 80906, (719) 576-2685. This group also has an excellent Web page with lots of information on individual unreached people groups at www.ad2000.org.

Gather teenagers back together, and say: **In spite of the efforts of nearly half a million missionaries in foreign countries, there are still people Christians call unreached. Unreached people are those who misunderstand or have no knowledge of Christ or the Gospels. Most of these people don't know about Christ because there are no active Christians who speak their languages to share the Word of God in ways they can accept and understand within their cultures. In other words, there are no Christian movements in their countries large enough to bring people to Christ.**

Some churches "adopt" groups of unreached people and try to help mission efforts in those countries. Other Christians make a point of praying for certain groups of unreached people.

One of these groups of unreached people is the Minang people group in West Sumatra, which is part of Indonesia. The Minang believe that Christians worship three gods: god the Father, god the Son, and god the Mother. Of the four million Minang people in West Sumatra, there are less than fifty Christians.

Another unreached people is the Tu group of China. They are Buddhists, and there are no known Christians among their nearly two hundred thousand people. It is estimated that 86 percent of the Tu people have never even heard the name Jesus Christ.

Non-Christians in the world today total nearly four billion, compared to fewer than two billion Christians. So it's clear to see that the world needs Jesus.

Let's take a moment to pray for these unreached people. Lead a short prayer of your own, or invite students to take turns praying aloud for the people in the world who don't know Jesus and the missionaries who are trying to bring them the gospel.

Say: **Now let's make a list of how our own church might support foreign missions.** On a sheet of newsprint, list ideas kids come up with. These might include writing to church-sponsored missionaries to find out more about their needs and to learn more about their daily lives; fund raising for a particular missions project; daily prayer for a certain missionary family; and gathering supplies to send in response to a request, such as clothing, school supplies, or Bibles.

REFLECTION AND COMMITMENT ▼

Comfort Zones (up to 10 minutes)
Say: **Probably very few of us will actually travel elsewhere in the world to do mission work. There are many mission needs right here in our own city and state. The term "global missions" encompasses the whole world, including the people right next door. Can you help me list some ideas for mission work here at home?**

On a sheet of newsprint, list ideas as kids brainstorm. Ideas might include volunteering time in a soup kitchen, homeless shelter, free medical clinic, or nursing home; helping with your church's vacation Bible

The World Is My Church 38

> # DEPTH FINDER — GLOBAL EVANGELIZATION
>
> The May 1996 issue of Current Thoughts & Trends shares the following quote from the National & International Religion Report (February 19, 1996):
>
> "In spite of the work of 4,500 missions agencies, 3,200 Christian broadcasting stations, and annual world missions expenditures of $10.5 billion, 20% of the world's population has yet to hear about Jesus Christ. If the present pace of evangelization continues, 16% of earth's inhabitants will still be without the gospel by the year 2000, the date by which many organizations hoped to complete the evangelization of the entire world."
>
> Sounds like we Christians have our work cut out for us. And the Bible says it won't be easy (Luke 10:2-3; Mark 16:15-18; John 15:18-21; and 2 Thessalonians 1:4).
>
> According to the Status of Global Mission 1997 report by David B. Barrett, there are nearly 2 billion Christians in the world. However, there are 1.1 billion Muslims, 886 million nonreligious people, 806 million Hindus, 328 million Buddhists, 224 million atheists, and so on, to total nearly 4 billion non-Christians in the world. In other words, of the estimated world population in 1997 of 5.8 billion, just 33.9 percent are Christians.
>
> The report also states that Christian workers total 4.7 million for all denominations, and foreign missionaries number 403,000.
>
> (Source for Status of Global Mission 1997 report: Global Evangelization Movement Web site: www.gem-werc.org.)

school or Sunday school classes; conducting clothing or food drives for needy people; adopting a child through Compassion International as a group; or committing to bringing friends (especially unchurched or non-Christian kids) to your youth group or class.

Ask:

● **How can you share your faith while doing these missions?**

● **What kinds of sacrifices might you have to make to do this service for God?**

Take the newsprint list of ways to support foreign missionaries the group created in the "True Stories" activity and the one listing ways to do mission work at home and hang them in front of the group for reference later in the "Power From the Spirit" activity.

Say: **Now, everyone stand up—we're going to do something fun. Line up** (pause as you direct kids to form a single file line), **and one by one, we're going to sing solos. Think about whether you'd rather sing the "Star-Spangled Banner" or "How Great Thou Art."** Pause while kids grumble or voice their objections. Then ask:

● **Does it make you uncomfortable to think about singing a solo?**

● **How might those feelings be like the way you might feel about sharing your faith?**

Say: **I asked you to sing solos to give you an idea of how it feels to step out of your comfort zone. To bring people to Christ or to spread God's Word, you often have to step out of your comfort zone, almost like singing a solo in front of a crowd of people.**

The World Is My Church

Often we fail to share our faith with others because we fear rejection, failure, or just sounding stupid. Ask:
- How do you motivate yourself to do something even if it makes you feel uncomfortable?
- How can you become comfortable doing something that was previously uncomfortable or scary?

Say: **Often we can expand our comfort zones by practicing what we feel uncomfortable doing, by taking lessons, by learning more about a subject, or even by praying for strength and power. I won't make you sing solos today. Instead, let's explore how you can become powerful as a witness of Christ's love so that you can share him with a <u>world that needs him</u>.**

"Then I heard the voice of the Lord saying,

'Whom shall I send? And who will go for us?'

And I said,

'Here am I. Send me!' "

—ISAIAH 6:8

DEPTH FINDER: CAN UNREACHED PEOPLE BE SAVED?

Your students might ask, "What about all those people who have never heard of Jesus Christ? Can they still gain eternal life?"

You'll probably have to tell them that you just don't know—no one knows!

According to The Quest Study Bible (Zondervan Publishing House), "the Bible is clear about the exclusive claims of Christ." John 14:6 states, "Jesus answered, 'I am the way and the truth and the life. No one comes to the Father except through me.'"

But we would like to think that a merciful and just God would not condemn those who, through no fault of their own, have never heard of him. "Salvation is always the result of God's love for us, not our love for him. It is his grace—not our efforts—that saves us," The Quest Study Bible reminds us.

Whatever God's plan is for those who have never heard of him, it's still a Christian responsibility to spread the gospel throughout the world (Matthew 28:19-20).

Power From the Spirit (up to 10 minutes)

Have kids sit back down in a large circle. In the center of the circle, place a few candles, light them, and then turn out the lights in the room.

Read aloud Acts 1:8 and Ephesians 6:19. Before you read each Scripture, give a short explanation. Tell students that Acts 1:8 relates the last words Jesus spoke before ascending into heaven and Ephesians 6:19 was written by Paul while he was imprisoned in Rome. After you've read both Scriptures, ask:

● **How does the Holy Spirit help us bring people to Christ?**
● **How can you be sure you are speaking the truth of the gospel when you're telling others about Christ?**
● **What are some ways you can get over the fear of sharing your faith or the fear of leaving your comfort zone when doing mission work?**

Say: **Let's form trios. Each trio needs to take a Bible and read Matthew 28:18-20.** Give each person paper and a pen (or give kids small journal books if you have these available). After trios have read the Scripture, have trios discuss the following questions. Have each person write his or her responses on a sheet of paper or in a journal. Ask:

● **What is the message of Matthew 28:18-20?**
● **What kinds of talents do you have that might help you do mission work at home or elsewhere in the world?**
● **What knowledge do you have to share with someone as a missionary at home or overseas?**

Say: **As we have seen, <u>the world needs Jesus</u>. The power and confidence to share Jesus with the world comes from the Holy Spirit. Let's take a few minutes in silent prayer and reflection. Think about whether God might want you to do mission work and if he does, what your response will be. Thank God**

LEADER TIP for Power From the Spirit

This activity is aimed at leading teenagers to commit to individual plans of action. But if you choose, you may commit as a group to a larger-scale project. For instance, if your group has the resources to take a mission trip out of your area, this might be a good time to commit to a project such as sponsoring a missionary family or needy child, attending a workcamp in the United States, or even planning a mission trip out of the country. Take this activity as far as you want to go, and remember the power of the Holy Spirit if your kids choose a project that might seem too big for your group.

LEADER TIP for Power From the Spirit

If you can't fully darken the room by pulling down shades or turning off lights, that's OK. Candles and quiet time will still help kids focus on the task.

LEADER TIP for Power From the Spirit

If some of your students are looking for a mission project that takes a firm commitment but not a lot of time, here's an idea. Turkish World Outreach has a unique project called Pen-Pals in Turkey. Turkey has a population of sixty million and is 99 percent Muslim. Open missionary activity is not allowed, and most of the people have never had the opportunity to talk with a Christian about the love of Christ.

Turkish World Outreach obtains the names of pen pals between the ages of thirteen and nineteen from English teachers in Turkey, and all correspondence is in English. Pen pals are matched by age group and common interests, and each Christian teenager receives guidelines to help him or her share the love of Christ effectively.

For more information, contact Don Mechem, Field Director, Turkish World Outreach, 508 Fruitvale Court, Grand Junction, CO 81504, (970) 434-1942.

for the power he has given you to understand and share his Word through the Holy Spirit, and pray for guidance in sharing Christ with the world.

After a few minutes, turn on the lights and blow out the candles.

Say: **Now let's make a commitment to mission work because <u>the world needs Jesus</u>.** Discuss with your trio members what you might like to do personally to contribute to global mission work. Refer to the two lists we made earlier, and make a commitment on your paper. Be sure to include the specific mission you will do and the time frame in which you'll complete your mission.

When teenagers have finished writing their commitments, have trio members affirm one another by encouraging each other to remember the power of the Holy Spirit as they complete their missions.

Encourage teenagers to keep journals of their mission experiences and to share mission projects with the church congregation to get other church members involved. You might also have weekly mission updates at your youth meetings, including sharing correspondence with missionaries or reporting progress on projects.

"Because of the service by which you have proved yourselves, men will praise God for the obedience that accompanies your confession of the gospel of Christ, and for your generosity in sharing with them and with everyone else."

—2 CORINTHIANS 9:13

The World Is My Church 42

DEPTH FINDER
MISSION RESOURCES

Whether your group chooses to do individual mission experiences close to home, support foreign missions, or actually plan a mission trip, there are many resources available to help you.

The Internet is full of Web sites focusing on global missions and includes directories of mission agencies, details of missionary needs, opportunities for youth mission trips, and details about unreached people.

Popular Internet search engines can point you to a variety of sites about Christian missions. Here are a couple of useful Web sites:

- Global Mapping International—www.gmi.org. This site is a treasure-trove of mission statistics, agencies, databases, and resources, and leads to numerous other mission Web sites. GMI also publishes the MARC North American Mission Handbook, which gives essential information about over nine hundred Protestant international mission agencies based in North America.
- Group Publishing, Inc. (Group Workcamps)—www.grouppublishing.com.

Group Publishing sponsors workcamps for teenagers throughout the country each summer.

Here are some addresses for a few of the larger mission agencies:

> Compassion International
> P.O. Box 7000
> Colorado Springs, CO 80933
> (719) 594-9900

> World Vision USA
> P.O. Box 9716
> Federal Way, WA 98063-9716
> (206) 815-2376

> Wycliffe Bible Translators
> P.O. Box 2727
> Huntington Beach, CA 92647
> (714) 969-4600

> Campus Crusade for Christ International
> 100 Sunport Lane
> Orlando, FL 32809-7875
> (407) 826-2000

And, of course, your own denomination's headquarters can share missionary information with your group.

Living the Faith

▼ GOD'S SMUGGLER

Mike had wanted to go to Asia since the night he heard a visiting missionary speak. He knew that God was doing something in his heart regarding missions and Asia, but he wasn't sure what. Mike found and read a copy of Brother Andrew's book *God's Smuggler*, and it changed his life.

Soon Mike found himself in the Shanghai airport with two suitcases full of Bibles he was smuggling into China. As he stepped off the plane, the humidity swept in like a thick blanket. People surged forward to disembark, dragging Mike with them. "It sure ain't Kansas, Toto," Mike thought.

Mike was with six team members, each carrying two suitcases of Bibles. The team members pretended they didn't know each other for safety reasons. The suitcases weighed sixty to eighty pounds each. The team had to pass checkpoints, guards, and ticket counters. No one in the group spoke Chinese, and no one at the airport spoke English. Mike had a knot in his stomach.

Once they got through the airport, all the suitcases were put in a cab and Mike, his teammate Diane, and their guide delivered the "bread." Pulling into a dark alley in Shanghai, they unloaded 1,200 pounds of Bibles and then went to find "Grandma." Grandma was eighty-two years old and famous all over China in the underground church because she had Bibles—the most precious thing a Chinese Christian can get. Once the Bibles were delivered into a corner of Grandma's apartment, she prayed silently over Mike and Diane, laying her hands on them. Mike and Diane were completely overwhelmed and wept for hours after the experience.

Mike's life was forever changed that night in Shanghai. Two days later, the team climbed aboard a train and headed for Hong Kong, embarking on another adventure.
—Kelly Johnson, Johnson Missionary Adventures and Christ for the Nations Institute

---

▼ A RUSSIAN CHRISTMAS STORY

Two Americans traveled to Russia in 1994 at the invitation of the Russian Department of Education to teach morals and ethics, based on biblical principles, in the public schools. At Christmastime, the missionaries visited a large orphanage where they planned to share the story of the Nativity with children who had never heard the story before. The children were fascinated by the Nativity story as they listened in wide-eyed amazement.

Afterward, the children were given bits of cardboard, napkins, and flannel to make crude mangers, and the missionaries gave them each a small baby Jesus cut from felt. One of the missionaries noticed that one young boy had placed two babies in his manger. Asked why there were two babies, the little orphan, Misha, began to repeat the Christmas story very seriously and accurately and then made up his own ending:

"And when Maria laid the baby in the manger, Jesus looked at me and asked me if I had a place to stay. I told him I have no mama and no papa, so I don't have a place to stay. Then Jesus told me I could stay with him," Misha said.

But Misha related that he had no gift for the baby and thought if he kept the baby warm, that would be a good gift.

"And Jesus told me, 'If you keep me warm, that will be the best gift anybody ever gave me.' So I got into the manger, and then Jesus looked at me and he told me I could stay with him—for always."

As little Misha finished his story, tears ran down his cheeks, he put his hands over his face, his head dropped to the table, and his shoulders shook as he sobbed and sobbed. The little orphan had found someone who would never abandon nor abuse him, someone who would stay with him—*for always!*

—Will Fish (submitted by Ken Keppel to Global Mapping International)

▼ HEALING FOR MARTA

During our first year in Bolivia, we began helping with a newly planted church that was made up of Quechua Indians from the Bolivian highlands. They were all very poor.

We noticed that one young girl had a badly deformed foot. She couldn't wear a shoe on that foot, and she walked with a limp. We asked people to pray for Marta and then took her to see some doctors. They told us they could do an operation to restore Marta's foot for six hundred dollars.

We contacted some friends in the States who sought help from their small group at church. A while later, we learned they had raised nine hundred dollars! Marta ended up needing two operations, and the extra money was enough to cover all of her medical expenses plus a new pair of tennis shoes.

What do you think Jesus would have done if he had met Marta during his earthly ministry? He would have healed her, right? I believe Jesus did heal Marta's foot; however, he did it through the faithfulness of his people.

—Dan and Arlene Cool, Charity Mission

▼ EASTER MIRACLE

Working as missionaries in the East Godavari district of Andhra Pradesh, India, James and Robbi Francovich visited the Yanadi village—made up of people from one of India's "untouchable" and "criminal" castes.

The two missionaries shook the people's hands, embraced them, told them about Jesus, and invited them to a Good Friday service and meal. Stunned by the kindness and the warmth of the Francoviches' touch, the untouchable Yanadi listened intently and then stunned the missionary couple in return—on Easter weekend, the entire village of fifty decided to reject Hindu idols and follow the God of the ones who came to see them! Never before, said Ramadu, the village elder, had anyone helped or loved them—much less touched them! "We were lost but now have found hope," he said. "We will go to church every Sunday."

On Christmas Day 1997, the members of the tribe were baptized together in the canal where they fish. Fifteen Yanadi children are receiving a Christian education, and the adults are learning to read and write in Telegu in preparation to read the Bible in their own language. Six adults have made the commitment to train to be evangelists to reach their own people for Christ.

—James and Robbi Francovich, Cooperative Baptist Fellowship (from an article by Robert O'Brien)

THE ISSUE: Persecution

TAKING UP THE CROSS

BY ERIN McKAY

Sharing in the Suffering of Christ

■ Suffering. It's a subject we don't like to *think* about, much less experience. In fact, most of us go to great lengths to make our physical and emotional existence as comfortable as possible. Compared to Christians in centuries past or Christians in some parts of the world today, those of us in the Western Hemisphere aren't subject to much suffering or persecution because of our faith. Yet we do sometimes suffer because of our beliefs if we imply through our words or actions that other people aren't living up to the standards Christ set for us. Our suffering may take the form of ridicule or ostracism, which is a particularly difficult prospect for kids who want so desperately to fit in and be liked by their peers. ■ If they are to be followers of Christ, it's important that kids be willing to stand up for what they believe, even if they have to take a little heat for doing so. God is counting on Christians to teach the rest of the world about Jesus, even though living out and sharing faith may sometimes cause personal suffering. ■ In this study, kids will be prompted to think about their willingness to share their beliefs when faced with possible conflict or ostracism. They'll learn why a loving God allows us to suffer and discover what the "up" side of suffering can be. Kids will gain an appreciation for the value of suffering when they realize that Jesus had to endure much greater suffering than they are asked to. And they'll be challenged to risk and accept suffering when it has the potential for leading others to our heavenly Father.

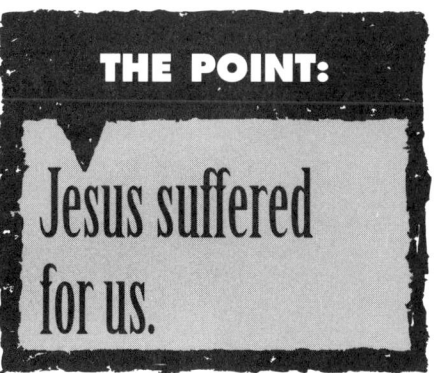

THE POINT: Jesus suffered for us.

The Study
AT A GLANCE

SECTION	MINUTES	WHAT STUDENTS WILL DO	SUPPLIES
Opening Experience	15 to 20	DECISIONS, DERISIONS—Listen to scenarios, choose a course of action for each scenario, and think about times they took a stand (or wish they had) for their beliefs.	Chalkboard or newsprint, chalk or a marker, tape, paper, pencils
Encountering the Word	20 to 25	ADMIRABLE ACTS—Examine early Christians' responses to persecution, compose and present psalms, and learn why and how we should share Christ with others even at the risk of persecution.	Bibles, "Admirable Acts" handouts (p. 55), pencils
Closing	10 to 15	SHARING FAITH AIN'T FOR WIMPS—Discuss their personal experiences with suffering because of their faith and create symbols to remind them of the Christian response to persecution.	Bibles; materials such as plastic foam, paper clips, and tape; papers from "Decisions, Derisions" activity

notes:

THE POINT OF "TAKING UP THE CROSS":

Jesus suffered for us.

THE BIBLE CONNECTION

PSALM 70	The psalmist responds to suffering by crying out to God.
ACTS 5:12-42; 6:8-10; 7:51-60; 12:1-17; 16:16-34	Many members of the early church were persecuted because of their faith in Christ.
2 CORINTHIANS 4:1, 5-7	Although we may suffer as Christians, God gives us the power to share his glory with others.
1 PETER 3:15-18	Christians should defend their faith "with gentleness and respect."

In this study, kids will examine scenarios in which they imagine themselves faced with choices that could result in suffering. They'll be asked to "take a stand" in response to each scenario, choosing between comfortable, less comfortable, and most uncomfortable courses of action.

They'll explore persecution suffered by the early Christians and discuss the Christian response to suffering because of beliefs.

Kids will then gain insight about the purpose of suffering and the ways in which we are to share our faith with others. They'll also make symbols that will remind them of the importance of sharing their faith, regardless of the cost.

Explore the verses in The Bible Connection and then examine the information in the Depthfinder boxes throughout the study to gain a deeper understanding of how these Scriptures connect with your young people.

BEFORE THE STUDY

On a chalkboard or a sheet of newsprint taped to a wall in your classroom, write "A" on the top left side. Toward the top center, write "B," and on the top right side, write "C." Make sure you leave plenty of space between the three choices.

On a table, set out materials for kids to use to create symbols in the "Sharing Faith Ain't for Wimps" activity.

LEADER TIP for The Study

Because this topic can be so powerful and relevant to kids' lives, your group members may be tempted to get caught up in issues and lose sight of the deeper biblical principle found in The Point. Help your kids grasp The Point by guiding kids to focus on the biblical investigation and discussing how God's truth connects with reality in their lives.

Taking Up the Cross   49

THE STUDY

OPENING EXPERIENCE ▼

Decisions, Derisions (15 to 20 minutes)

After kids have arrived, direct them to the middle of the room and point out the three letters on the wall. Ask kids to listen to the following situations and decide which of the three courses of action they would most likely take in each situation. Explain that when they have made their decisions, they are to go to the board and take their places near the letters that correspond with the choices they've selected.

Say: **Scenario One: You are walking through the mall when you pass a group of kids sitting on a bench. One of them tosses a bag of fast-food trash in the potted-plant display behind him and sees you watching. You would (A) walk by, but give him a dirty look; (B) pick up the bag and put it in the nearest trash can; or (C) stop in front of him and say, "There's a garbage can right over there. If you don't want to put your trash in it, I will." Then pause to see what he does.**

Wait for students to move to A, B, or C, indicating the course of action they would take.

Then say: **Scenario Two: You are sitting in the school cafeteria with a group of classmates, and they start talking negatively about someone in one of your classes. Although you are shocked by what you hear and doubt that it's true, the information is intriguing. You would (A) not say anything, and resolve to keep the rumor to yourself; (B) tell the subject of the rumor what's being rumored; or (C) express that you don't feel right talking about people behind their backs. If the gossip continues, quietly get up and leave.**

Pause while students make their choices.

Say: **Scenario Three: Your best friend, Dave, and his girlfriend, Janice, have been dating each other exclusively for several months, but on Saturday night you happen to see Janice holding hands with another guy. When you see him on Monday, Dave comments that he and Janice don't keep any secrets from each other. You would (A) not mention what you saw on Saturday night; (B) let Janice know in a roundabout way that you saw her on Saturday night; or (C) pick an appropriate place and time to ask Dave if Janice has told him about the guy you saw her with on Saturday night.**

Wait for students to make their choices.

Say: **Scenario Four: Someone in your history class got the answers to the final exam, and the list is being passed around. You would (A) refuse to look at the list, and continue studying for the**

Leader TIP for Decisions, Derisions

Some approaches to sharing faith are more effective than others, depending on circumstances, personalities, and the depth of one's convictions. There are times a Christian feels compelled to express a belief, even if doing so results in conflict. At other times, Christian faith sharing might be more effective when a more passive approach is used. (A person who quietly makes the Christlike choice in a difficult situation can make a very strong impression.) As kids grapple with the choices presented in the scenarios, make sure they understand that option C is not necessarily always the *right* one to select. In fact, the appropriateness or effectiveness of choosing option C might be an interesting topic for discussion as you bring this activity to a close.

Taking Up the Cross   50

exam; (B) send the teacher an anonymous note letting him or her know about the list; or (C) tell your classmates that a good grade on the exam won't mean anything if you have to cheat to get it, and that you'll have to let the teacher know the answers are going around.

Wait for students to make their choices.

Say: **Scenario Five: An English course at your school has been gaining in popularity ever since the teacher started taking her classes to the Shakespeare festival and making the field trip an overnighter. The teacher doesn't realize it, but a lot of underage drinking goes on during these field trips. Sure enough, during the trip you attend, your roommate sneaks a case of beer into your hotel room, and kids start filing in. You would (A) not make an issue of it; (B) call the instructor from the lobby, and tell her there's a great party going on in room 313; or (C) take your roommate aside, tell him or her you feel uncomfortable with the beer in your room, and ask him or her to take the party elsewhere.**

After kids have made their choices, ask:

● **Why is it hard to speak up sometimes, even when you know you're right?**

● **Which of these options (A, B, or C) would make you the most uncomfortable?**

● **If you were to choose the most uncomfortable option in each of these scenarios, what might be some *positive* outcomes?** (You might need to read the scenarios and options aloud again so kids can come up with ideas.)

● **Do you see any similarities between the suffering that Christ endured and the suffering you might have to go through if you chose option C in any of these scenarios? Explain.**

Give each person a pencil and a sheet of paper, and say: **I'd like you to take a moment to think of a time you suffered for standing firm in a particular conviction and doing what you thought was right. If you can't think of a time you spoke up (or stood firm) and consequently suffered, think instead of a time you wish you had spoken up but instead kept quiet. Write what you thought of on your sheet of paper, fold it in half, and hold on to it until later.**

LEADER TIP for Decisions, Derisions

If kids have a hard time thinking of personal experiences of suffering, be prepared to tell about a time you were treated badly or felt discomfort because of your beliefs.

DEPTHFINDER — SILVER LININGS

According to the Bible, clouds of suffering contain a number of silver linings. For example, suffering draws us to God (2 Corinthians 7:8-10); can glorify God (1 Peter 4:1-2); prepares us for joy to come (1 Peter 4:12-13); and makes us better people (James 1:2-4 and 1 Peter 5:10). The Bible also promises that God will bless those who suffer for doing good things (Matthew 5:10 and 1 Peter 3:13-14). You might want to ask kids to find other biblical references to the positive effects of suffering.

Taking Up the Cross   51

LEADER TIP for The Study

Whenever groups discuss a list of questions, write the questions on newsprint and tape the newsprint to the wall so groups can discuss the questions at their own pace.

Today we're going to think and talk about suffering, especially as it pertains to living and sharing our faith. We know that Jesus suffered for us. In trying to help people understand God, it was necessary for Jesus to expose their sin, and so Jesus brought anger and suffering on himself. The people who choose to follow Christ often risk persecution because of their belief in him. Let's look at the experiences of some of Christ's followers.

ENCOUNTERING THE WORD ▼

Admirable Acts (20 to 25 minutes)

Say: **In this next activity, you're going to write a psalm. Does everyone know what a psalm is?** Make sure that kids understand that a psalm is a poem or a song used in worship, then read aloud Psalm 70 to give them a specific example.

Say: **Although this particular psalm was written many years before the earliest Christians began to be persecuted, the psalm writer was feeling in need of God's protection and strength just as persecuted Christians may feel. I'm going to ask you to take a look at some Christians who stood firm in the face of persecution. Then I want you to compose psalms on their behalf. Put yourselves in their shoes, and write psalms that sound like ones they might have written. It's OK to use modern, everyday language.**

Divide the kids into four groups, and number the groups from one to four. Give each group one copy of the "Admirable Acts" handout (p. 55) and a pencil. Ask each group to look up its assigned Bible passage and then compose a psalm to God written from the viewpoint of the main character or characters in the passage. Groups can write their psalms on the back of their handouts.

Say: **The psalms you compose should be about the characters' suffering and should communicate the answers to the questions on the handout.**

After about fifteen minutes, ask someone from each group to read the group's psalm aloud. When all of the groups have read their psalms, ask for a round of applause. Then ask:

● **Why do you think the Christians we read about in Acts were allowed to suffer?**
● **How did they respond to their persecution?**

Have someone read 1 Peter 3:15-18 aloud. Then ask the entire group:

● **What do these verses say about sharing Christ with others?**
● **Why did Jesus suffer for us?**

Read aloud 2 Corinthians 4:1, 5-7, then ask:

● **In what ways does God give us power to withstand suffering for his name?**
● **According to this passage and the passage in 1 Peter, how should we respond to suffering?**
● **How can our response to persecution bring others to Christ?**

Say: **Whenever we are facing persecution, it's important to remember that Jesus suffered for us.** His suffering was not only physical but emotional as well. The Bible says that Jesus was *rejected* by the very people he had come to save. Eventually, he was also *deserted* by those who had followed him! Jesus faced persecution to bring us into a right relationship with God, but it has also been suggested that Jesus suffered to teach us how to suffer. In his book, *Cry, the Beloved Country,* Alan Paton says, "I have never thought that a Christian would be free of suffering. For our Lord suffered. And I have come to believe that He suffered, not to save us from suffering, but to teach us how to bear suffering. For He knew that there is no life without suffering." Ask:

- What do you think Jesus' life can teach us about suffering?

Say: You may have heard the expression that someone has "aged gracefully." Well, Jesus is someone who *suffered* gracefully. He was able to do so because he trusted in the wisdom and goodness of his heavenly Father and understood his own purpose in the world. In the hours just before he was arrested and crucified, Jesus prayed, "My Father, if it is not possible for this cup to be taken away unless I drink it, may your will be done." Jesus chose not to try to escape suffering but to suffer gracefully. You cannot escape suffering during this lifetime. But you can suffer gracefully if you understand your purpose and remember that God's opinion of you is the one that matters.

> *"Bless those who persecute you; bless and do not curse."*
>
> —**Romans 12:14**

Taking Up the Cross

DEPTH FINDER: NO PAIN, NO GAIN?

In his book *Where Is God When It Hurts?*, Christian author Philip Yancey points out that suffering is necessary for growth and even joy. "Most worthwhile human accomplishments involve a long history of struggle," he writes. "Would the pleasure be possible without the painful process?

"There's a corollary to the pain/pleasure principle in the Christian concept of service. The genius of Christianity is that true fulfillment is found, not through comfortable ego-fulfillment, but through painful, tedious service.

"Happiness will come upon me unexpectedly, as a by-product, a surprising bonus for something I have invested myself in. And, most likely, that investment will include much pain."

Yancey points out that suffering often produces something; for example, athletes and expectant mothers put up with suffering in return for a desired outcome. But the most important reason for suffering, according to Yancey, is that it draws people to the Lord: " 'Pain turned you to God'—in my view, this is probably the most accurate, succinct summary of the role of suffering. It blends with the Bible's tone of emphasizing the Christian's response, not the cause of the suffering."

CLOSING ▼

Sharing Faith Ain't for Wimps

(10 to 15 minutes)

Say: **Now I'd like you to look back at what you wrote on your paper at the beginning of our study. Think about what you've learned today about the reasons we suffer and the way God calls us to respond to persecution. Find a partner, and tell him or her about your personal example of suffering. If you feel you would have handled the situation differently if you had applied the advice found in the Bible passages, tell your partner what you would have done differently.**

Give pairs a few minutes to share, then have pairs reread 1 Peter 3:15-18 together. Say: **Now I'd like each of you to use the materials I've set out to create a symbol that represents the meaning of this Scripture. Make it something that will remind you of the reason we are called to suffer for our faith and the way we should respond to persecution.** Give kids a few minutes to create their symbols, then ask volunteers to share their symbols with the group. Ask kids to bow their heads to close in prayer. Pray: **Dear God, whenever we feel persecuted, remind us that <u>Jesus suffered for us</u>, and that if we, too, are willing to speak up, it is possible to bring others to you. Give us the courage to share our faith with others, even if it makes us uncomfortable. In our most difficult moments, give us the strength and confidence to suffer gracefully. In Jesus' name we pray, amen.**

Admirable Acts

Look up the passage, answer the questions below, and use your answers to compose a psalm to God based on the character's or characters' point of view.

Group One—*Acts 5:12-42*
Group Two—*Acts 6:8-10; 7:51-60*
Group Three—*Acts 12:1-17*
Group Four—*Acts 16:16-34*

- *Who* did the suffering in this particular passage?

- *How* did that person (or persons) suffer?

- What did that person (or persons) *do* to bring on the suffering?

- How did that person (or persons) *respond* to the suffering?

Permission to photocopy this handout from Group's Core Belief Bible Study Series granted for local church use.
Copyright © Group Publishing, Inc., P.O. Box 481, Loveland, CO 80539.

why ▼ Active and Interactive Learning works with teenagers

Let's Start With the Big Picture

Think back to a major life lesson you've learned.
Got it? Now answer these questions:
- Did you learn your lesson from something you read?
- Did you learn it from something you heard?
- Did you learn it from something you experienced?

If you're like 99 percent of your peers, you answered "yes" only to the third question—you learned your life lesson from something you experienced.

This simple test illustrates the most convincing reason for using active and interactive learning with young people: People learn best through experience. Or to put it even more simply, people learn by doing.

Learning by doing is what active learning is all about. No more sitting quietly in chairs and listening to a speaker expound theories about God—that's passive learning. Active learning gets kids out of their chairs and into the experience of life. With active learning, kids get to *do* what they're studying. They *feel* the effects of the principles you teach. They *learn* by experiencing truth firsthand.

Active learning works because it recognizes three basic learning needs and uses them in concert to enable young people to make discoveries on their own and to find practical life applications for the truths they believe.

So what are these three basic learning needs?
1. Teenagers need action.
2. Teenagers need to think.
3. Teenagers need to talk.

Read on to find out exactly how these needs will be met by using the active and interactive learning techniques in Group's Core Belief Bible Study Series in your youth group.

1. Teenagers Need Action

Aircraft pilots know well the difference between passive and active learning. Their passive learning comes through listening to flight instructors and reading flight-instruction books. Their active learning comes

Helpful Stuff   57

through actually flying an airplane or flight simulator. Books and lectures may be helpful, but pilots really learn to fly by manipulating a plane's controls themselves.

We can help young people learn in a similar way. Though we may engage students passively in some reading and listening to teachers, their understanding and application of God's Word will really take off through simulated and real-life experiences.

Forms of active learning include simulation games; role-plays; service projects; experiments; research projects; group pantomimes; mock trials; construction projects; purposeful games; field trips; and, of course, the most powerful form of active learning—real-life experiences.

We can more fully explain active learning by exploring four of its characteristics:

● **Active learning is an adventure.** Passive learning is almost always predictable. Students sit passively while the teacher or speaker follows a planned outline or script.

In active learning, kids may learn lessons the teacher never envisioned. Because the leader trusts students to help create the learning experience, learners may venture into unforeseen discoveries. And often the teacher learns as much as the students.

● **Active learning is fun and captivating.** What are we communicating when we say, "OK, the fun's over—time to talk about God"? What's the hidden message? That joy is separate from God? And that learning is separate from joy?

What a shame.

Active learning is not joyless. One seventh-grader we interviewed clearly remembered her best Sunday school lesson: "Jesus was the light, and we went into a dark room and shut off the lights. We had a candle, and we learned that Jesus is the light and the dark can't shut off the light." That's active learning. Deena enjoyed the lesson. She had fun. And she learned.

Active learning intrigues people. Whether they find a foot-washing experience captivating or maybe a bit uncomfortable, they learn. And they learn on a level deeper than any work sheet or teacher's lecture could ever reach.

● **Active learning involves everyone.** Here the difference between passive and active learning becomes abundantly clear. It's like the difference between watching a football game on television and actually playing in the game.

The "trust walk" provides a good example of involving everyone in active learning. Half of the group members put on blindfolds; the other half serve as guides. The "blind" people trust the guides to lead them through the building or outdoors. The guides prevent the blind people from falling down stairs or tripping over rocks. Everyone needs to participate to learn the inherent lessons of trust, faith, doubt, fear, confidence, and servanthood. Passive spectators of this experience would learn little, but participants learn a great deal.

● **Active learning is focused through debriefing.** Activity simply for activity's sake doesn't usually result in good learning. Debriefing—evaluating an experience by discussing it in pairs or small groups—helps focus the experience and draw out its meaning. Debriefing helps sort and order the information students gather during the experience. It helps learners relate the recently experienced activity to their lives.

The process of debriefing is best started immediately after an experience. We use a three-step process in debriefing: reflection, interpretation, and application.

Reflection—This first step asks the students, "How did you feel?" Active-learning experiences typically evoke an emotional reaction, so it's appropriate to begin debriefing at that level.

Some people ask, "What do feelings have to do with education?" Feelings have everything to do with education. Think back again to that time in your life when you learned a big lesson. In all likelihood, strong feelings accompanied that lesson. Our emotions tend to cement things into our memories.

When you're debriefing, use open-ended questions to probe feelings. Avoid questions that can be answered with a "yes" or "no." Let your learners know that there are no wrong answers to these "feeling" questions. Everyone's feelings are valid.

Interpretation—The next step in the debriefing process asks, "What does this mean to you? How is this experience like or unlike some other aspect of your life?" Now you're asking people to identify a message or principle from the experience.

You want your learners to discover the message for themselves. So instead of telling students your answers, take the time to ask questions that encourage self-discovery. Use Scripture and discussion in pairs or small groups to explore how the actions and effects of the activity might translate to their lives.

Alert! Some of your people may interpret wonderful messages that you never intended. That's not failure! That's the Holy Spirit at work. God allows us to catch different glimpses of his kingdom even when we all look through the same glass.

Application—The final debriefing step asks, "What will you do about it?" This step moves learning into action. Your young people have shared a common experience. They've discovered a principle. Now they must create something new with what they've just experienced and interpreted. They must integrate the message into their lives.

The application stage of debriefing calls for a decision. Ask your students how they'll change, how they'll grow, what they'll do as a result of your time together.

2. Teenagers Need to Think

Today's students have been trained not to think. They aren't dumber than previous generations. We've simply conditioned them not to use their heads.

You see, we've trained our kids to respond with the simplistic answers they think the teacher wants to hear. Fill-in-the-blank student workbooks and teachers who ask dead-end questions such as "What's the capital of Delaware?" have produced kids and adults who have learned not to think.

And it doesn't just happen in junior high or high school. Our children are schooled very early not to think. Teachers attempt to help kids read with nonsensical fill-in-the-blank drills, word scrambles, and missing-letter puzzles.

Helping teenagers think requires a paradigm shift in how we teach. We need to plan for and set aside time for higher-order thinking and be willing to reduce our time spent on lower-order parroting. Group's Core Belief Bible Study Series is designed to help you do just that.

Thinking classrooms look quite different from traditional classrooms. In most church environments, the teacher does most of the talking and hopes that knowledge will transmit from his or her brain to the students'. In thinking settings, the teacher coaches students to ponder, wonder, imagine, and problem-solve.

3. Teenagers Need to Talk

Everyone knows that the person who learns the most in any class is the teacher. Explaining a concept to someone else is usually more helpful to the explainer than to the listener. So why not let the students do more teaching? That's one of the chief benefits of letting kids do the talking. This process is called interactive learning.

What is interactive learning? Interactive learning occurs when students discuss and work cooperatively in pairs or small groups.

Interactive learning encourages learners to work together. It honors the fact that students can learn from one another, not just from the teacher. Students work together in pairs or small groups to accomplish shared goals. They build together, discuss together, and present together. They teach each other and learn from one another. Success as a group is celebrated. Positive interdependence promotes individual and group learning.

Interactive learning not only helps people learn but also helps learners feel better about themselves and get along better with others. It accomplishes these things more effectively than the independent or competitive methods.

Here's a selection of interactive learning techniques that are used in Group's Core Belief Bible Study Series. With any of these models, leaders may assign students to specific partners or small groups. This will maximize cooperation and learning by preventing all the "rowdies" from linking up. And it will allow for new friendships to form outside of established cliques.

Following any period of partner or small-group work, the leader may reconvene the entire class for large-group processing. During this time the teacher may ask for reports or discoveries from individuals or teams. This technique builds in accountability for the teacherless pairs and small groups.

Pair-Share—With this technique each student turns to a partner and responds to a question or problem from the teacher or leader. Every learner responds. There are no passive observers. The teacher may then ask people to share their partners' responses.

Study Partners—Most curricula and most teachers call for Scripture passages to be read to the whole class by one person. One reads; the others doze.

Why not relinquish some teacher control and let partners read and react with each other? They'll all be involved—and will learn more.

Learning Groups—Students work together in small groups to create a model, design artwork, or study a passage or story; then they discuss what they learned through the experience. Each person in the learning group may be assigned a specific role. Here are some examples:

Reader

Recorder (makes notes of key thoughts expressed during the reading or discussion)

Checker (makes sure everyone understands and agrees with answers arrived at by the group)

Encourager (urges silent members to share their thoughts)

When everyone has a specific responsibility, knows what it is, and contributes to a small group, much is accomplished and much is learned.

Summary Partners—One student reads a paragraph, then the partner summarizes the paragraph or interprets its meaning. Partners alternate roles with each paragraph.

The paraphrasing technique also works well in discussions. Anyone who wishes to share a thought must first paraphrase what the previous person said. This sharpens listening skills and demonstrates the power of feedback communication.

Jigsaw—Each person in a small group examines a different concept, Scripture, or part of an issue. Then each teaches the others in the group. Thus, all members teach, and all must learn the others' discoveries. This technique is called a jigsaw because individuals are responsible to their group for different pieces of the puzzle.

JIGSAW EXAMPLE

Here's an example of a jigsaw.

Assign four-person teams. Have teammates each number off from one to four. Have all the Ones go to one corner of the room, all the Twos to another corner, and so on.

Tell team members they're responsible for learning information in their numbered corners and then for teaching their team members when they return to their original teams.

Give the following assignments to various groups:

Ones: Read Psalm 22. Discuss and list the prophecies made about Jesus.

Twos: Read Isaiah 52:13–53:12. Discuss and list the prophecies made about Jesus.

Threes: Read Matthew 27:1-32. Discuss and list the things that happened to Jesus.

Fours: Read Matthew 27:33-66. Discuss and list the things that happened to Jesus.

After the corner groups meet and discuss, instruct all learners to return to their original teams and report what they've learned. Then have each team determine which prophecies about Jesus were fulfilled in the passages from Matthew.

Call on various individuals in each team to report one or two prophecies that were fulfilled.

You Can Do It Too!

All this information may sound revolutionary to you, but it's really not. God has been using active and interactive learning to teach his people for generations. Just look at Abraham and Isaac, Jacob and Esau, Moses and the Israelites, Ruth and Boaz. And then there's Jesus, who used active learning all the time!

Group's Core Belief Bible Study Series makes it easy for you to use active and interactive learning with your group. The active and interactive elements are automatically built in! Just follow the outlines, and watch as your kids grow through experience and positive interaction with others.

> **FOR DEEPER STUDY**
>
> For more information on incorporating active and interactive learning into your work with teenagers, check out these resources:
>
> ● *Why Nobody Learns Much of Anything at Church: And How to Fix It,* by Thom and Joani Schultz (Group Publishing) and
> ● *Do It! Active Learning in Youth Ministry,* by Thom and Joani Schultz (Group Publishing).

your evaluation of

Bible Study Series
for senior high

why SHARING FAITH matters

Group Publishing, Inc.
Attention: Core Belief Talk-Back
P.O. Box 481
Loveland, CO 80539
Fax: (970) 679-4370

Please help us continue to provide innovative and useful resources for ministry. After you've led the studies in this volume, take a moment to fill out this evaluation; then mail or fax it to us at the address above. Thanks!

● ● ● ● ● ●

1. As a whole, this book has been (circle one)

not very helpful   very helpful
1   2   3   4   5   6   7   8   9   10

2. The best things about this book:

3. How this book could be improved:

4. What I will change because of this book:

5. Would you be interested in field-testing future Core Belief Bible Studies and giving us your feedback? If so, please complete the information below:

Name _____

Street address _____

City _____ State _____Zip _____

Daytime telephone (____) _____ Date _____

THANKS!